Michelle Yeoh

A Little Golden Book® Biography

By Angela Song
Illustrated by Irene Chan

A GOLDEN BOOK • NEW YORK

Text copyright © 2025 by Angela Song
Cover art and interior illustrations copyright © 2025 by Irene Chan
All rights reserved. Published in the United States by Golden Books, an imprint of
Random House Children's Books, a division of Penguin Random House LLC, 1745 Broadway,
New York, NY 10019. Golden Books, A Golden Book, A Little Golden Book, the G colophon,
and the distinctive gold spine are registered trademarks of Penguin Random House LLC.
rhcbooks.com
Educators and librarians, for a variety of teaching tools, visit us at RHTeachersLibrarians.com
Library of Congress Control Number: 2024940874
ISBN 978-0-593-81331-7 (trade) — ISBN 978-0-593-81332-4 (ebook)
Printed in the United States of America
10 9 8 7 6 5 4 3 2 1

Michelle Yeoh was born Yeoh Choo Kheng on August 6, 1962, in Ipoh, a large city in Malaysia. Her mother was a housewife, and her father was a lawyer.

Her family spoke English and Malay, the official language of Malaysia. Michelle also spoke Malaysian Cantonese with her grandmother.

As a child, Michelle was full of energy and loved to try new things. She played basketball and piano and was on a diving team. She was also the Malaysian junior squash champion!

But her true love was dance. Michelle began studying ballet at the age of four. She dreamed of one day being a ballerina.

When she was fifteen, Michelle and her parents moved to England so she could study ballet at the Hammond, a school for the performing arts.

After training at Hammond, Michelle made the move to the Royal Academy of Dance in London. She practiced every day and worked hard to make her dream come true.

But in her last year at the Royal Academy, Michelle injured her spine during a rehearsal. The doctor told her she would never be able to dance professionally.

Michelle had to change her plans. She enrolled in college and took some acting classes, but she had stage fright and couldn't remember her lines. Becoming an actress didn't seem possible.

When Michelle graduated college, she wasn't sure what she would do next.

Michelle considered opening a ballet school in her hometown. But when she returned to Ipoh, she discovered that her mother had secretly entered her in the Miss Malaysia beauty pageant. Michelle didn't want to be in a beauty contest, but competed to make her mom happy.

To her surprise, Michelle won and was crowned Miss Malaysia! After that, she entered more pageants around the world.

In 1984, Dickson Poon, a Hong Kong businessman who ran a jewelry company, was looking for the perfect person to star in a commercial for his fancy watches. Michelle went to Hong Kong to meet Dickson right away.

Michelle got the part! She appeared alongside an action-movie star named Jackie Chan. That commercial was her first acting job, and it caught the attention of filmmakers in Hong Kong. They wanted Michelle to be in their movies!

At first, Michelle was cast as the "damsel in distress," or the woman who needed to be rescued. But she didn't want to be saved. She wanted to jump off buildings, fight villains, and be the hero!

Michelle trained hard to learn how to do her own stunts. Soon, she convinced filmmakers that she could be an action hero, too. In 1985, she had her first starring role as a police officer in the film *Yes, Madam!* For this movie—and others that she made in Hong Kong—she used the stage name Michelle Khan.

After making three more movies, Michelle decided to take a break from acting. She and Dickson had fallen in love, and in 1988, they got married. She wanted to focus on being a wife and mother.

Sadly, Michelle soon learned she was unable to have children. A few years later, she and Dickson ended their marriage, but they remained good friends.

Michelle started acting again. She was offered a role in *Police Story 3: Supercop.* The action movie starred Jackie Chan—the actor she met when she filmed her first commercial!

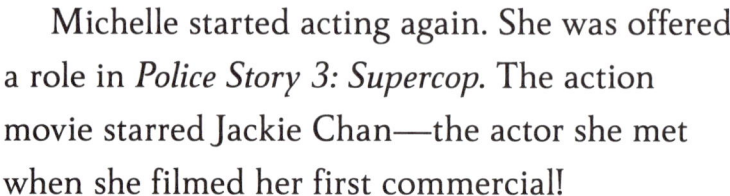

Just like Jackie, Michelle performed all her own stunts in the film. During one scene, she jumped from the top of a truck onto a moving car. She fell off, but then she got right back up and did it again. Jackie was impressed.

The movie was a big success and led to more movie offers for Michelle. She quickly became one of Hong Kong's most famous actresses. It wasn't long before filmmakers in Hollywood wanted her in their movies, too.

In 1997, Michelle made her Hollywood debut in the James Bond movie *Tomorrow Never Dies.* Her character, Wai Lin, was a fighter and a hero, just like James Bond! As always, Michelle did all her own stunts, even when the director thought it might be too dangerous.

Once in Hollywood, she changed her name back to Michelle Yeoh.

Tomorrow Never Dies was a box-office hit. Michelle got lots of new job offers, but she turned many of them down. She didn't want roles that she felt relied on Asian or female stereotypes. She had always played strong, powerful women and wanted to take on similar roles again.

Michelle waited two years for that perfect part to come along. In 2000, she starred in the Chinese martial arts film *Crouching Tiger, Hidden Dragon*. Her character, Yu Shu Lien, was a great and honorable warrior in nineteenth-century China.

The film was in Mandarin, a language Michelle didn't know how to speak. But she refused to let someone else dub over her voice. Michelle learned her lines by memorizing the way the words sounded.

After the success of *Crouching Tiger, Hidden Dragon*, Michelle starred in many popular Hollywood movies. She also appeared on the TV series *Star Trek: Discovery* as Captain Philippa Georgiou.

In 2018, Michelle played Eleanor in *Crazy Rich Asians.* Her character wasn't very nice—she didn't want her son to marry a young woman from a different background than her own. Because Eleanor was an overbearing mother, Michelle worried her character would be seen only as an Asian stereotype. She carefully portrayed Eleanor as a strong woman who was proud of her Asian traditions and values but who still had a lot to learn from the younger generation. Audiences loved the movie and her performance.

Michelle's martial arts background came in handy
in the Marvel film *Shang-Chi and the Legend of the Ten
Rings* and also in *Everything Everywhere All at Once*.
Michelle's character in that fantasy-adventure movie
discovers she's a kung fu master in a different universe.

It was one of Michelle's biggest roles—and it
changed her life!

The movie won many awards, including an Oscar for Best Picture. And Michelle became the first Asian woman ever to win the Oscar for Best Actress! Her win was important not just for Michelle but for the many Asian filmmakers in Hollywood who were finally getting recognized for their work.

When she's not acting, Michelle spends time with her family. In 2023, she married Jean Todt and became a stepmother to his son, Nicolas. She is godmother to one of her first husband's daughters and has four other godchildren, too. Michelle often returns to Ipoh to visit with her family back home.

Michelle is also active in many charities. She is a member of the International Olympic Committee and a United Nations Development Programme Goodwill Ambassador. She supports conservation groups like Save China's Tigers. In 2009, she worked with National Geographic to make the film *Among the Great Apes,* a documentary that shows how endangered orangutans are protected in her home country of Malaysia.

Michelle's path to achieving her goals wasn't always easy or what she expected. But she never lost her love of trying new things. By standing up for what's important to her and never giving up, Michelle became the hero of her own story!